Breaking Through to the Next Level

by
Zig Ziglar

Honor Books
Tulsa, Oklahoma

Breaking Through to the Next Level
ISBN 1-56292-495-8

3330 Earhart, Suite 204
Carrollton, Texas 75006-5026

Published by Honor Books, Inc.
Box 55388
Tulsa, Oklahoma 74155

Introduction

In *Breaking Through to the Next Level* I want to encourage you to be more and do more than you ever thought possible. I have filled this handy training tool with quotes, definitions, and illustrations that have inspired me on my own journey to a new level.

Breaking Through to the Next Level covers all areas of life—business, relationships, goal setting, happiness, child training, and more—because you can't have true success in life if one area is lacking. It takes a whole, balanced life to truly make an impact on the world around you.

This book is designed to be accessible. You can easily read the whole book in one sitting, read a few pages every morning, or a couple of pages on a break. Whichever method you choose, you'll want to read it more than once. I believe it will motivate and inspire you afresh each time you pick it up.

I always say, "You can get everything in life you want, if you help enough other people get what they want," and this book can do just that—help people get what they want. So keep extra copies on hand to give to friends and colleagues. Help them get what they want, and I'll see you at the next level!

Success is one thing you can't pay cash for. You've got to buy it on the installment plan and make payments every day.

Everybody has his or her own definition of success. Here's mine: "When you have achieved a balance in your personal, family, and business life by a maximum utilization of your abilities which has brought rewards to you in your physical, mental, and spiritual realms, you are successful."

How do you achieve success? Combine the right attitude with specific skills, add the Golden Rule philosophy and a specific game plan. Now build your life on a character base and you have an excellent chance of achieving total success.

Children have never been very good at listening to their elders, but they've never failed to imitate them.

—James Baldwin

Recently my wife and I were in our favorite yogurt store. As we ate, our attention was drawn to a father and his two beautiful little girls. They were teaching their father the "Macarena." The older one would demonstrate to the younger one and her dad exactly how the dance went. The dad would get confused, and the little girls would laugh with delight.

Chances are good that when he gets to be an old man they will treat him lovingly, because he treats them lovingly now. What we sow is what we reap.

If you already have that loving situation in your family, I hope you're grateful for it.

The quality of a person's life is in direct proportion to their commitment to excellence, regardless of their chosen field of endeavor.

It's my observation that what we do off the job plays a major role in how far we will go on the job. For example, if one hour each day were taken from watching television and spent in acquiring a new skill, reading some inspirational information, getting involved in study groups, learning a foreign language, teaching a functionally illiterate how to read—anything that would make you know you're capable of doing worthwhile things—you would feel better about life and about yourself. This increases your effectiveness on the job and in dealing with life in general.

You can't make the other person feel important in your presence if you secretly feel that he is a nobody.

—Les Giblin

Several years ago I received this letter: "Dear Zig: My name is Scott Allen. I met you at the Roswell Street Baptist Church this year. I am twelve years old. You looked at me and turned me around and checked me over. You said, 'Yes, I can see you're going to be a winner.' I want to let you know how I am doing. My grades are better and my teacher likes me more. I guess I am going to be a winner. I have lots of friends now. Thank you for caring. I will see you at the top! Love, Scott Allen."

I have studied the lives of great men and famous women and I found that the men and women who got to the top were those who did the jobs they had in hand with everything they had of energy, enthusiasm, and hard work.

—*Harry S. Truman*

Surely every schoolboy in America knows the story of Abe Lincoln and the trials he went through before he became president of the United States. Most people also have the seeds of greatness within them, but for whatever reason they're never inspired, encouraged, or committed to doing anything with what they have. Yet opportunity lies around us in many strange and interesting forms. Everything starts somewhere and every company in the world, regardless of its size, started first in the mind of one person who shared it with others who caught the dream.

You must start somewhere, so start where you are.

**The mediocre teacher tells;
the good teacher explains;
the superior teacher demonstrates;
the great teacher inspires.**

—William Arthur Ward

My first-grade teacher, Mrs. Dement Warren, taught me to read. My sixth-grade teacher, Mrs. J. K. Worley, taught me to love to read. I'm convinced parents should let their children see them reading good books, magazines, and articles. Children are great imitators. If they see their parents wrapped up in a good book instead of glued to the television set, they are likely to follow suit. In addition, read good books to your kids. Please consider it, parents. Show your love for reading and your kids will do the same.

Of all the "attitudes" we can acquire, surely the attitude of gratitude is the most important and by far the most life-changing.

Dr. Jack Graham points out that each person in his or her lifetime will cultivate either an attitude of thanksgiving and gratitude, or an attitude of bitterness and arrogance. He expands on this by pointing out that a grateful child is far more likely to be a happy child. Conversely, a person who is angry and critical is basically unhappy.

Gratitude will not only make you healthy and happy, it will also change your perspective in life. Happy people primarily focus on others; unhappy people focus on themselves and wallow in self-pity and doubt. Grateful people are far more optimistic and see whatever circumstances they're in as an opportunity for good.

Sometimes we all need to realize that negative thoughts have no power. We empower them.

—Kurt Goad

I love the story of the hobo who climbed aboard a railroad car just at dusk, and in a moment or two one of the railroad personnel came by and closed the door, locking it from the outside. Later, the unwelcome guest discovered he was in a refrigerator car, and he was deeply concerned. As the car got colder and colder, his imagination started to work overtime. He started to shiver.

The next morning, when the refrigerator car was opened, the dead tramp was discovered inside. The interesting fact is the lowest temperature that had been reached in the car the night before was 55 degrees.

Forgiving means to pardon the unpardonable. Faith means believing the unbelievable. And hoping means to hope when things are hopeless.

—G. K. Chesterton

Lanny Thomas is the enthusiastic executive director of the Dallas Life Foundation in Dallas, Texas, which is committed to taking homeless people off the streets. Lanny says, "I once believed that all homeless people needed was to learn a skill or get a job. However, my experience taught me that help is important but hope is imperative."

Anyone who believes his or her problems are permanent and unsolvable will give up easily. That's an inside problem, not a skill problem. If a person believes that problems are temporary and specific, they are optimistic about their future and continue trying to overcome life's difficulties.

Don't be distracted by criticism. Remember—the only taste of success some people have is when they take a bite out of you.

It's generally true that few statues have ever been erected in a critic's honor, and yet critics play a vital role in our society. The role they play is important, because they do things for us that our friends will seldom, if ever, do. They point out our shortcomings and our faults. Sometimes we're unaware of them; the critic helps us to identify them.

You can depend on it. Anybody who ever does anything of significance, regardless of the field of endeavor, is going to be criticized. The way the successful ones handle that criticism is the reason they are successful.

Our business in life is not to get ahead of others, but to get ahead of ourselves, to break our own records, to outstrip our yesterday by our today.

—Stuart B. Johnson

On Saturday afternoon, December 14, 1996, I attended one of the most exciting athletic events of my life. It was the State 5A Championship Game between the Lewisville Fighting Farmers and the Converse-Judson Rockets. Even though I was pulling for the Converse-Judson Rockets and they eventually lost by twenty-four points, those young men didn't know the word "quit."

They simply gave it everything they had from beginning to end. The winners were gracious in victory; and the beaten team, while totally disappointed, were equally gracious as they congratulated the victors. They left the field with heads held high, convinced that next year will produce different results. That's class.

We make our decisions based on our fundamental beliefs and character qualities.

Today we have a "not my fault" society. It appears that when something goes wrong, the culprit invariably says, "It's not my fault."

I love this little analogy. One man gets nothing but discord from the keys of a piano; another gets harmony. No one claims the piano is at fault. Life is the same way. The discord is there—so is the harmony. Play it correctly, and it gives forth beauty; play it falsely, and it will utter ugliness. But life is not at fault. The trouble lies in the player. When we accept responsibility for our future, our future will be much brighter.

A big man is not one who makes no mistakes, but one who is bigger than any mistakes he makes.

Many times "accidents" are not really accidents, but fortuitous events brought about by a strange series of circumstances that produce an entirely unexpected result. The key to all of this is being receptive and open-minded. Just because something comes out differently doesn't necessarily mean it's spoiled or ruined. Many recipes of great value and delightful taste have come about because somebody "fouled up" the mixture of ingredients and came up with a delicious new product.

When an accident happens and it appears that all is lost, carefully examine the results. You can't undo the "mistake," so analyze it carefully—you never know what you might come up with!

**The true and noble way
to kill a foe is not to kill him.
You, with kindness, may so
change him that he shall cease
to be a foe and then he is slain.**

—Alayn

The 1828 Noah Webster Dictionary says that to forgive is to "overlook an offense and treat the offender as not guilty." Forgiving our enemies is considered a Christian duty. In reality, forgiveness is something you do for yourself. Many people rightfully argue that their offender does not "deserve" to be forgiven. That is entirely beside the point. You deserve to forgive that individual.

It is impossible to go as high as you're capable of going if you're carrying the burden of hate, revenge, and bitterness. Those are heavy loads to carry, and the chances of you realizing your full potential are nonexistent with those three burdens on your back.

You can't change the past but you can ruin a perfectly good present by worrying about the future.

—*Decision*

We can get downright negative if we focus on the failures of the past, the issues we face today, and the fear of what's going to happen tomorrow. That approach to life will not only shorten our life span, but it will make our life seem unbearably long because we're concentrating on what is bad.

Try this simple approach: Start with the fact that if you're reading this you obviously are alive. You did wake up this morning. Then, concentrate on the pleasant, positive experiences you've had. Based on my own experience, and the experiences hundreds have shared with me over the years, this shift in focus works wonders.

We are told that talent creates its own opportunities, but it sometimes seems that intense desire creates not only its own opportunities, but its own talents.

—Eric Hoffer

Doug Blevins has spent his entire life flat on his back in bed or enthusiastically tooling around in his wheelchair. Though Doug has never taken a step or kicked a football, he is the kicking coach for the Miami Dolphins.

It's important to also note that Doug recognized as a child, thanks to his parents, that he could not run and kick; but that he could think, study, plan, prepare, and expect. Parents, I encourage you to teach Doug's approach to your kids. Under his parent's guidance Doug did all those things and that's why today he's successful.

Dedicated people have "Employment Security."

Before coming to work for the Zig Ziglar Corporation, my son-in-law was a superintendent for one of the nation's largest home builders. In five years of working for them, he was never late for work. He was excited about his job, and consistently gave more than a full day's effort for a full day's pay.

Those actions and attitudes built real job security. Realistically, however, there are some things that people can't control despite their best efforts. But consider this: If his company had suddenly gone under, what kind of recommendation do you think he would have gotten from his employer?

Won't developing those same qualities give you employment security?

Your birth, which obviously happened despite the odds of over millions to one, means you became a winner before you were born. One sperm "saw" one egg, took off in hot pursuit, made the connection, and you were on your way.

— James Parker

To get to the next level, you have to plan to win. The good news is, you were off to a great start even before you were old enough to make choices. Your arrival was well-planned eons ago. Your mother and father may not have specifically planned on having you, and they may have thought your timing wasn't quite right. But I assure you, you are the winner you were meant to be.

Never again will you face such apparently insurmountable odds. You've already won the big one; you are already the right person.

Recognize your mistakes and learn from them, but don't dwell on them.

In virtually every case, you are what you are and where you are because of the choices which you have made or which have been made for you. Accidents do happen and assaults do occur, but they are the exception rather than the rule.

A few weeks ago a young woman was lamenting the fact that her two marriages had failed. She was feeling quite low, so I reminded her that in her lifetime she had made thousands of good choices and at least two poor ones. That offered no instant cure, but it did make her think. I'm hopeful she will build on those thoughts.

He who has done his best
for his own time
has lived for all times.

—Johann Von Schiller

Several years ago the Big Ten Football Conference did a study on the difference between winning football teams and losing teams. The bottom line was clear: The difference between the first place and second place team was the difference in length of total effort. The average player went all-out two and seven-tenths seconds on every play. The difference between the team that finished first versus the team that finished last was nine-tenths of a second spent in all-out effort. The difference between first and second place was five-tenths of a second in total effort.

Consistently giving your best effort will make you a winner.

**The foundations of character
are built not by lecture,
but by bricks of good example,
laid day by day.**

One day my son walked into the bathroom while I was shaving. He looked at my hair and said, "Dad, what happened to your hair?" I explained that I had spilled some of my shampoo in the sink and had put that shampoo on my hair, since I would be showering in a few moments. My son said, "Dad, no one could ever accuse you of wasting anything."

It is my conviction that parents should take advantage of everyday situations to teach their children certain principles, so I smiled at my son and said, "Son, your nice little Ford Thunderbird was bought because we take care of 'little things.'"

You can't give character to another person, but you can encourage him to develop his own by possessing one yourself.

—Artemus Calloway

The Center for Creative Research did a study on people who make it all the way to the top in their fields. They discovered that once a trust is broken because of a character flaw, that individual has built a glass ceiling on how high he or she can go in that organization.

A person with character and integrity is always in demand in the marketplace, because they can be taught the necessary skills. When we combine the positive qualities of character and integrity with the specific skills necessary to get the job done, we've got an individual whose future is bright indeed. Yes, character does count.

The only difference between a big shot and a little shot is that a big shot is just a little shot that kept on shooting.

All of us have heard someone described as a "natural-born salesman," or that he or she was "born with" a talent. There's no denying that some people start off with more talent than others. However, a five-year study of 120 of the nation's top artists, athletes, and scholars has concluded that drive and determination, and not great natural talent, led to their extraordinary success.

The most brilliant mathematicians often said they had trouble in school and were rarely the best in their classes. Researchers interviewed the families and teachers of these super-achievers and consistently heard accounts of their extraordinary drive, dedication, and hard work. There is no substitute for tenacity.

Hope is not passive—
it is an active attitude.

One morning, while sitting with my wife, enjoying my favorite breakfast, it dawned on me why I am happy virtually all of the time. My life is filled with great expectations. I had looked forward to that pancake breakfast since we spotted the IHOP the night before, so I anticipated the enjoyment that would be mine.

A Harvard University study revealed that people who attend a seminar with great expectations get the most out of it. Oftentimes they don't get everything they expect but, as compensation, many times they get many things they did not expect. The same "expectation" principle applies to all of life.

It's not so important to be serious as it is to be serious about important things.

—Robert M. Hutchins

A good sense of humor is a real asset in the social and business world. We enjoy being around people who can laugh at funny situations or themselves, yet who take life—not themselves—seriously. The dictionary says that humor is "that quality of the imagination which gives to ideas a wild or fantastic turn, and tends to excite laughter or mirth by ludicrous images or representations." Humor makes a man ashamed of his follies without exciting his resentment.

A healthy sense of humor enables us to laugh with people and not at them. And we know that a good laugh is healthy, both physically and emotionally.

If you are wearing out the seat of your pants before you do your shoe soles, you're making too many contacts in the wrong place.

—*Anonymous*

What do Darren Woodson of the Dallas Cowboys, Terrell Davis of the Denver Broncos, and Simeon Rice of the Phoenix Cardinals have in common? Each of these three outstanding football players has received considerable honor as players. Why? Because they are extremely hard workers. They all put in extra effort that causes them to excel. This work ethic is something all of us can have.

These outstanding athletes accomplished their objectives because they work extraordinarily hard and always participate more as team players than for individual honors. That's a good approach to take in life.

We all get two gifts we should use as much as possible—imagination and humor. Imagination compensates us for what we are not; a sense of humor consoles us for what we are.

An interesting quote by actress Janet Leigh recently appeared in the Dallas Morning News. She said her blood-curdling screams in the famous shower scene of the movie *Psycho* were just a case of good acting and not cold water as some people believed. The fascinating part is the fact that acting in the scene did not frighten her, because she could see and feel and know exactly what was happening. However, when she later saw the scene in the movie, it so frightened her that from that time on she has only taken baths.

The imagination is powerful. That's why we should turn our thoughts in a positive direction.

You are only one—but you are one, and one person can make a difference.

One voice in the wilderness might not turn the wilderness into productive farmland, and yet if you add enough voices to the one, marvelous things can happen. Think about it: General Motors started in the mind of one man, as did IBM, General Electric, and all other companies and businesses. One person has an idea and sells it to another; soon there are several people enthusiastic about a project, and things begin to happen. One highly-motivated citizen can organize a neighborhood group and have a dramatic impact on crime.

Don't discount the impact your one voice can make.

The ocean of possibilities is enormously inviting, yet terribly threatening. For most of us the problem is not a lack of potential, it's a lack of perseverance; not a problem of "having the goods," but of "hearing the bads."

—*Jay Strack*

The Jay Leno approach is one I like. When he replaced Johnny Carson on *The Tonight Show*, he started to take some heat. Critics unfavorably compared him to Johnny, and from all that criticism most people thought his stay as the host would be short-lived. Realistically speaking, however, Jay never really worried. In fact, the record shows that he kept a stack of unpleasant reviews on his desk for inspiration. One critic said, "Too many soft questions." Another said, "He's being too nice." These unkind words didn't bother Leno, though, because they were written in 1962 and were directed at Jack Paar's replacement—"an awkward nobody named Johnny Carson."

Vision—it is essential for survival. It is spawned by faith, sustained by hope, sparked by imagination, and strengthened by enthusiasm. It is greater than sight, deeper than a dream, broader than an idea. Vision encompasses vast vistas outside the realm of the predictable, the safe, the expected. No wonder we perish without it. Ask God to stretch your vision today.

—Chuck Swindoll

In 1991 a group of investors came up with a novel idea. After the NCAA championship game was played in Indianapolis, they invested $65,000 in buying the floor on which the final four games were played. They cut this brand new basketball court into 22,000 little pieces.

These investors sold those little 6x5-inch pieces of floor to 22,000 fans as souvenirs for $24.95 each. This creativity turned their $65,000 investment into $548,900 in less than a week. Those opportunities are everywhere and we need to recognize them and take action. So, keep your eyes open, let your imagination work, and be open to new concepts.

Time flies.
It's up to you to be the navigator.

—Robert Orben

One of the ironies of life is that somehow we find time to do things over when we didn't have time to do them right the first time. When it gets down to the absolutely "gotta-do-it-right" time, most responsible people will do exactly that. Had they invested a few more minutes initially, they could have saved themselves time and trouble. "I'll take care of this when I have more time," knowing full well that an inordinate amount of time has already elapsed. Think about it—not when you have time, but right now. Then take action—not when something else happens, but right now.

**Circumstances and situations do color life,
but you have been given the mind
to choose what the color shall be.**

—John Homer Miller

The most successful people in the world have been confronted with countless failures. Eddie Arcaro lost over 300 races before he notched his first win, and yet he became one of the greatest jockeys in history. Oprah Winfrey lost her first job as a television anchorwoman, and her next show was pulled off the air. Today she's applauded around the world for her successes.

The question is, how do we respond to failure? Do we ask, "Why me?" or take the Arthur Ashe approach and say, "If I don't ask 'why me' after my victories, I cannot ask 'why me' after my setbacks and disasters."

Habits are about the only servants that will work for you for nothing. Just get them established and they will operate even though you are going around in a trance.

—*Frederick Whitaker*

Input determines outlook, outlook determines output, and output determines outcome. Fortunately, we can choose what to feed our minds by reading good materials, watching educational, inspirational video tapes, or listening to informational audio tapes in the car.

If life isn't giving you what you want, a change of thinking might be the solution. If we keep on thinking what we've been thinking, we will keep on doing what we've been doing; and if we keep on doing what we've been doing, we will keep on getting what we've been getting. So, make your mental diet a positive one. A diet change like that will make a permanent difference.

When I am employed and serving others,
I do not look upon myself as
conferring favors but
paying debts.

—Benjamin Franklin

While working as the sales manager for Disney Radio, Pam Lontos was approached by a salesman who wanted her job and wanted her to teach him how to do it. She did, and she was promoted to vice president for sales.

People who train their replacements, who promote others up to their level, are viewed with considerable enthusiasm by upper management. Because leadership and management are always needed, those who can develop others are far more likely to move up the ladder than those who simply "do their job." Take that approach. Share your knowledge and information, and inspire others to do better. Teach them what you know.

America is only another name for opportunity.

—Ralph Waldo Emerson

The son of Australian immigrants, Richard Fisher says, "On every national holiday, this son wakes up early in his comfortable house, takes out his American flag and posts it on his front porch. Alone in the twilight before sunrise, he says a prayer, thanking God and the Founding Fathers for creating a nation that would take in and nurture immigrants possessing nothing more than hopes and ambitions.

"America is the only place on Earth where a half-Aussie, half-Norwegian African almost-Mexican American can thrive." He says, "There is no such thing as a hyphenated American. Fifty years ago, we cast our hyphens to the winds and never looked back."

This is an age in which one cannot find common sense without a search warrant.

—George F. Will

I'm persuaded that most of the problems we encounter in life can be easily and quickly handled with a quiet, simple, common-sense question or observation concerning the issue.

Many times we send for help when, as somebody said, the solution to most problems lies at the end of our sleeve. It's in our own hands. Think about it. Take the simple steps of not jumping to conclusions and get to the heart of the matter with one or more simple questions. Many times you will find the solution.

Motivation is the fuel necessary to keep the human engine running.

Regularly someone will tell me that when they get "a little bit down," they plug in a tape and it invariably gives them that lift they need. My question is always, "Why would you wait until you get 'down'? Why not make it a way of life, so that as you drive you automatically plug in some words of encouragement?" It's easier to stay "up" than it is to get "up." Additionally, motivation is most beneficial when we are already inspired. Then when we fuel the motivational engine, we will come up with more creative ideas.

He who has a thousand friends has not a friend to spare, while he who has one enemy shall meet him everywhere.

—Ralph Waldo Emerson

Everyone speaks of the need for friends and the role they can play in their lives, but an anonymous writer put it this way: "Friends in your life are like pillars on your porch. Sometimes they hold you up and sometimes they lean on you. Sometimes it's just enough to know they're standing by." Elisabeth Foley points out that friendship doubles our joy and divides our grief and that the most beautiful discovery true friends make is that they can grow separately without growing apart.

Friendship requires many things—unselfishness, genuinely caring for the other person, and listening when they need to talk. Friendship is priceless.

Only the curious will learn and only the resolute overcome the obstacles to learning. The quest quotient has always excited me more than the intelligence quotient.

—Eugene Wilson

One of those immutable laws says that a body at rest will tend to remain at rest until and unless it is acted upon by some force. That force can be internal or external. If we wait for the external, it might never happen. That's the reason we need to "take the bull by the horns," seize the moment, develop a plan of action, decide what we want out of life, and pursue that plan until something happens. Interestingly enough, even if we fail to accomplish the objectives we set, we will be infinitely better off in the seeking than we can possibly be in the waiting.

A good criterion for measuring your success in life is the number of people you have made happy.

—Robert J. Lumsden

The dictionary says that happiness is "the agreeable sensations which spring from the enjoyment of good; that state of being in which desires are gratified." It's "the enjoyment of pleasure without pain."

My 1828 Noah Webster Dictionary says, "The pleasurable sensations derived from the gratification of sensual appetites render a person temporarily happy, but he only can be esteemed really and permanently happy who enjoys peace of mind and the favor of God."

Other people can give you pleasure, but you will never be happy until you do something for someone else. Happiness comes not only from being the right kind of person but also from doing things that benefit others.

You seldom come across anything more enjoyable than a happy person.

—Frank Clark

It's my conviction that one cannot be a happy person without a little pleasure in life. For most people, pleasure is important.

Here's a yardstick you need to use before you indulge in any pleasure: "Can I repeat this pleasure indefinitely and be happy?" If the answer is "no," you want to be wary of indulging in that pleasure.

Greta Palmer wisely observed, "Those only are happy who have their minds on some object other than their own happiness—on the happiness of others, on the improvement of mankind, even on some art or pursuit followed not as a means but as itself an ideal end."

Success is peace of mind in knowing you did your best.

—John Wooden

According to psychologist Carol Dweck, youngsters who are told their good work reflects high intelligence "learn to measure their intelligence by their performance"; then when they encounter setbacks they falter in discouragement. However, according to Ms. Dweck, "Kids who are taught that effort is the key to success keep trying after failures."

When a child makes an "A" on the test, it is of long-term benefit to say, "I know you've worked hard for that grade, not only on your homework but with your classroom habits, too. I'm proud of you for that."

Praise your kids for effort, not their "smarts." Lifetime habits will be formed, producing lifetime winners.

Input influences outlook, outlook influences output, and output determines outcome.

—Anonymous

Music has always had an influence in our lives. Andrew Fletcher, a great Scottish patriot, wrote in 1702, "You write the laws, let me write the music, and I will rule your country." Fletcher was obviously saying that the words put into your mind affect your thinking, your thinking affects your actions, and your actions produce results—some good, some not so good.

What goes into your mind through conversation, reading, observing, listening, etc., influences your behavior. To quote speaker Bill Chaffin, "When you listen to the wrong voices you will make the wrong choices, and when you listen to the right voices you will make the right choices."

When you change your world for the better, you have positioned yourself perfectly to change the world of those around you.

A moment's reflection will remind us that virtually none of us gets overly excited when we're confronted with a "problem." However, those who solve problems are the ones who survive and thrive. And the more problems we solve, the greater our value to the company and customer, and the higher our rewards.

The people who receive the highest recognition and rewards are those who are not only capable of solving problems but also have the foresight and ability to prevent problems before they arise. Think carefully about things that could be a problem in the future. Head them off; solve them before they occur. You'll be rewarded.

By listening, by caring, by playing you back to yourself, friends ratify your better instincts and endorse your unique worth. Friends validate you.

—Gail Sheehy

As certainly as the night follows the day we all need and desire help or companionship—or both. Accidents, illness, tragedies, boredom, loneliness, or all of the above are a fact of life. During those times friends can literally be lifesavers.

Friends also make good times better and not only increase our enjoyment of life but also contribute to our health and happiness.

Question: "How do you make friends?" Answer: Start with simple things—a pleasant smile, a cheerful, upbeat, positive attitude, gracious manners—all attract favorable attention, and that's the first step to getting acquainted. Once acquainted, you are in position to cultivate a friendship.

**Don't trust the experts.
You can't always go by expert opinion.
A turkey, if you ask a turkey,
should be stuffed with
grasshoppers, grits, and worms.**

—Anonymous

I'm always intrigued with the number of "unbreakable" records which continue to be broken. The truth is, records are made to be broken—maybe by you.

I suspect that all of us, at one time or another, have been told we couldn't do something only to learn later that with commitment, preparation, and intense effort, we could do far more than even we had imagined. Don't always listen to the "experts"—listen to your heart. Give it your best shot. Even if you don't make it all the way you will still have "won," because giving your best effort *always* makes you a winner.

**We have committed
The Golden Rule to memory,
now let's commit it to life.**

The most unusual fight to ever take place easily occurred in the '30s. In this match, C. D. Blalock was knocked out in an unheard-of twist of events. He took a swing at his rival but ended up hitting himself. His punch missed the intended target and collided with his own face.

Strange story? Yes, but perhaps there is a strong message here for each of us. How many times do we self-destruct by losing our temper, being rude to people who genuinely love us and, for that matter, to strangers? Treat other people like you want to be treated and you will dramatically reduce your chances of self-destructing.

**You can't turn back the clock,
but you can wind it up again.**

—Bonnie Prudden

Suppose you had daily invested a few more minutes studying and increasing your knowledge in your chosen profession. How many more friends would you have had had you been a little more courteous, thoughtful, and considerate? How much more energy and vitality would you have had had you developed better eating habits, exercised regularly, and gotten the right amount of sleep? How much happier would you have been had you spent more time with your family?

As you think about these things, just remember that you still have time to do many of the above. Why not go ahead and get started?

Reality tells us that your biggest task, your biggest objective, should be not to get ahead of others but to use your own ability to increase your own performance.

Once George Bernard Shaw was approached by a reporter who said, "Mr. Shaw, you are internationally famous and have traveled all over the world. You've been around some of the most famous people and you're on a first-name basis with royalty, well-known authors, artists, teachers, and dignitaries. If you had your life to live over and could be anybody you've ever known, who would you want to be?"

"I would choose," replied Shaw, "to be the man George Bernard Shaw could have been but never was."

Real success is measured by what you have done compared to what you could have done with the ability God gave you.

The best way to make a difference in others' lives is to make changes in our own.

For some strange reason a very high percentage of us believe those around us should change, and not us. It's our mate's fault, our employer's fault, the government's fault, the school's fault, or society's fault. Many people honestly believe all that would have to happen for them to become enormously successful and completely happy would be for the people around them to change.

Consider for a moment all the people between the ages of twelve and fourteen who believe their parents are completely out of touch. We know by the time they reach the age of twenty-five they will be amazed at how much their parents have learned!

I never knew a man who was good at making excuses who was good at anything else.

—Benjamin Franklin

My mentor, retired businessman Fred Smith, says, "You are the way you are because that's the way you want to be. If you really wanted to be any different, you would be in the process of changing right now." It probably will not surprise you when I say that I am in complete agreement with Fred. He's the wisest man I've ever known and combines wisdom with common sense, a unique sense of humor, and a willingness to help others accomplish their objectives. Fred points out that change, while often difficult, is one of the necessary ingredients in life if we are to succeed or, for that matter, even survive.

First, a new theory is attacked as absurd. Then it is admitted to be true, but obvious and insignificant. Finally, it is seen to be so important that its adversaries claim they themselves discovered it.

—*William James*

I'm certain all of us have watched with envy as some simple idea has brought fame and fortune to its originator. Haven't we all heard somebody say, "I thought of that!"

Philosopher Alfred North Whitehead made this observation: "Almost all new ideas have a certain aspect of foolishness when they are first produced. The history of science is full of examples. Copernicus said the earth revolves around the sun. Louis Pasteur said disease is caused by microscopic creatures called 'germs.' Newton spoke of an invisible force called 'gravity.' These scientists could have been top comedians in their day just by standing on a stage and reciting their theories."

Parents who wonder where the younger generation is going should remember where it came from.

—*Sam Ewing*

A wit once said that we should "train up a child in the way he should go and go there ourselves once in a while." Obviously, that's good, sound advice.

It has been rightly observed that we teach people what we know, but we reproduce what we are. It's true that people might not always believe everything we say, but they will believe everything we do.

Whether you are a parent, educator, politician, employer, manager, etc., keep in mind that your most effective and important job is the growth, development, and inspiration you can pass on to others, particularly those in your direct charge.

Liberty is the right to discipline ourselves in order not to be disciplined by others.

—*Clemenceau*

The sales person who keeps records will sell substantially more merchandise than the sales person who does not. However, the sales person who knows not only what happened, but why it happened, and how he can utilize that information to his benefit, will sell considerably more. Knowing the "why" makes it possible to take care of the "how" and lessens the sales person's inclination to kid himself or herself about why results are not better.

Regardless of what you're doing in life, understand that if you know what you want and have a plan of action to get there, you're far more likely to reach whatever objective you have set.

Wise sayings often fall on barren ground, but a kind word is never thrown away.

—Sir Arthur Helps

"You're a great little wife, and I don't know what I would do without you." And as he spoke he kissed her, and she forgot all the care in that moment. And forgetting it all, she sang as she washed the dishes and sang as she made the beds. The song was heard next door, and a woman there caught the refrain and sang also. Now two homes were happier, because he had told her that sweet old story—the story of the love of a husband for a wife.

So, because he kissed her and praised her, the song came and the influence went on and on.

We all find time to do what we really want to do.

—William Feather

Listen in on virtually any conversation today and eventually the subject of people being so busy they no longer have any free time will come up. Unfortunately, most people honestly believe that is true. However, according to Geoffrey Godbey, "People constantly underestimate their free time and overestimate their work hours. They're in denial."

According to the experts, free time is actually on the rise. The question is, "What is happening to our time?" For every extra hour of free time Americans have gained, they spend an extra hour watching television. Purely and simply, it's the lack of direction, not the lack of time, that creates the problem.

Laughter is the shortest distance between two people.

—*Victor Borge*

Once when our oldest granddaughter (who is now twenty) was a two-year-old, she was crying about something. I suspected she was merely trying to get more attention, so I stepped into the kitchen and called out, "Waaaiiit a minute, Sunshine! Don't shed another tear!" Then, carrying a large mixing bowl toward her, I said to her, "Sunshine, those tears are so valuable. I don't want to lose a single one. Let's collect them in this mixing bowl and perhaps we can sell them to the neighbors. Now, cry real good for me, Sunshine!" Interestingly enough, her tears quickly turned to laughter.

The Constitution only guarantees the American people the right to pursue happiness. You have to catch it yourself.

—Benjamin Franklin

Less than 1 percent of all millionaires in America are professional athletes or entertainers. The overwhelming majority of those who become wealthy do it the old-fashioned way. They get an education, start at the bottom of the ladder, and slowly, over a period of time, make their way to the top. Along the way they continue to hone their skills, live within their means, and invest their money wisely. They live a lifestyle that requires they deny themselves some of the things they want now, so they can acquire the things they really want later in life. The best way to acquire wealth is the old-fashioned way—you earn it.

**Monuments! What are they?
The very pyramids have forgotten
their builders or to whom
they were dedicated. Deeds, not stones,
are the true monuments of the great.**

—John L. Motley

A young man about thirty-five years old was having dinner with his father who was probably in his sixties and had apparently suffered a stroke. His speech was slurred and his movements were labored. As I watched, I was moved by the gentle, loving, patient, compassionate way the young man talked with his father. He showed him every attention and was obviously delighted to be with his dad.

Later I had a chance to speak to the son. I commended him for his patience and love for his dad. He thanked me and responded that his father, all of his life, had treated him in the same way.

What comes out of your mouth is determined by what goes into your mind.

Our society today is more negative than positive. Our conversations at home accentuate the negative. Unfortunately, a negative thinker activates the world around him negatively, and every bit of negativism he sows produces a bumper crop. Albert Einstein said we have to have seven positive influences to overcome one negative one.

Change emphasis—change results. Take one day and after each encounter jot down the gist of the conversation. I promise you, by the end of the day your comments will be more positive than they were at the beginning. Once we become aware of what we are doing, the solution is on its way.

Our deeds determine us as much as we determine our deeds.

—*George Elliott*

Life really is like a bouncing ball. What you send out is what you get back. According to Dr. J. Allan Petersen, the finest gift we can give another human being is the gift of an excellent expectation. He says that "expecting the best provides realistic affirmation of a person's uniqueness, individuality, and strengths, and it multiplies itself. It encourages a reciprocal action from other people. The Biblical principle, 'Give and it shall be given unto you,' applies to expressing appreciation."

This is simply another way of using the Golden Rule in our everyday lives, and that is to treat other people the way you want to be treated.

Wisdom is the correct use of the truth in the knowledge which we have.

—Fred Smith

We now are roughly doubling information and knowledge every two years. And yet, despite this fact, most people would agree that we have more problems than ever before. The question then: "Is knowledge and information the answer?" The answer is obviously "no."

Some wise person said that knowledge is knowing, but wisdom is knowing what to do with it. Someone else has said that knowledge is proud that it knows so much; wisdom is humbled that it knows so little. And Dr. Adrian Rogers says, "You need knowledge to pass the tests in school; you need wisdom to pass the tests of life."

Forgiveness is not an elective in the curriculum of life. It is a required course and the exams are always tough to pass.

At a recent convention I spoke on the fact that forgiveness is the vital key in ridding ourselves of hate, anger, and bitterness caused by abuse.

The next morning a woman came to me and told me her story. Her stepfather had sexually abused her. She had not spoken with him in ten years. She left my presentation the night before and called him. When he heard her voice, he was stunned. She told him that not only had she forgiven him, but that she loved him. As she told her story, there was a radiance about her and a beautiful smile on her face that clearly said she was free.

I have never met an unhappy giver.

—George Adams

Dr. Michael Guillen says that deep down happiness comes from deep-rooted, intimate relationships like being married or believing in God, and also from a deep-seated conviction that life has a purpose worth pursuing. Dr. Richard Davidson of the University of Wisconsin says that "happiness is the process associated with achieving our goals."

This is confirmed by a study done by David Jensen at UCLA which showed that people with specific goals and plans for reaching them are not only happier and healthier, but they also get along better with people at home and make more money.

When you return to your boyhood town, you find it wasn't the town you longed for—it was your boyhood.

You know you're getting older when everything hurts and what doesn't hurt doesn't work . . . you sit in a rocking chair and can't get the thing moving . . . your knees buckle but your belt won't . . . you feel like "the morning after" even when you didn't go anywhere.

Having said all those things, let's take a look at the research. Researchers studied the lives of 400 famous people and discovered that 66 percent of their major accomplishments occurred after age sixty. Unfortunately, many people retire with their best years in front of them. Keep on working. You'll be healthier, happier, and live longer.

No one can go back and start a new beginning, but anyone can start today and make a new ending.

—Anonymous

Ralph Waldo Emerson's definition of success: "Finish every day and be done with it. You have done what you could. Some blunders and some absurdities no doubt crept in. Forget them as soon as you can. Tomorrow is a new day. Begin it well and serenely with too high a spirit to be cumbered with your old nonsense. This day is all that is good and fair. It is too dear, with its hopes and invitations, to waste a moment on the yesterdays." Good advice.

Remember that failure is an event and not a person. Yesterday really did end last night. Today is a brand new day.

Those who make it big have had their share of failures, so the next time you're knocked flat just smile and say, "I'm certainly in good company. Now I'm ready to move up."

My favorite saying about failure is: "Failure is a chance to start over," so we should get excited about problems. Duke Ellington says "A problem is a chance for you to do your best."

My own research reveals that the only way to the mountaintop is through the valleys, because the valleys of life are where we develop the strength and creativity for the climb to the top.

Realistically, most of us don't get overly excited about failures. However, when failures come our way, if we look at them with the right attitude, they truly can become "makers" instead of "breakers."

Happiness, like success and love, is not a destination but a lifelong journey.

From the *Philippine Observer,* come these steps to being happy: Happiness cannot be caused by someone else; it is not done to you or for you. Happiness is a choice.

Happiness is a result of effective living. Happiness is not a reward; it is a consequence.

Happy people are those who focus on what is important—other people. That might be the secret to happiness in old age right there—being loving and being loved.

You will experience happiness only as you experience more life. More living means, among other things, more accomplishment; the attainment of worthwhile goals; more happiness for both yourself and others.

Happiness is not something you experience, it's something you remember.

—Oscar Levant

Happiness is not a "when" and a "where"; it is a "here" and "now." You will not be happy when you win the trip to Hawaii, when you get the promotion, when you move into the new house, when the kids go to school, etc.

The key is taking inventory of the things you should be happy about now: your health, your spouse, your neighborhood, your freedom, your education, etc. List the things you're happy about at this moment. Then you will come to the realization that you have much to be happy about now, and that will dramatically improve your chances of being even happier in the future.

Things turn out the best for those who make the best of the way things turn out.

Tom Dempsey was born with only half a right foot and a deformed right hand. Fortunately, his parents never made him feel uncomfortable with his "handicap." As a result, Tom did everything his buddies did as he was growing up. As a youngster he discovered that his natural ability lay in kicking the football. For him, that was good because his "handicap" did not prove to be a handicap.

Tom tried out for the New Orleans Saints, and the coach's skepticism was overcome by Tom's enthusiasm. Two weeks later, Tom Dempsey kicked a fifty-five-yard field goal in an exhibition game and earned a spot on the roster.

Successful people tell others how to get on, not where to get off.

We all smile with delight when someone who is "always right" makes a dogmatic statement and then has to "eat their own words." However, what is the right thing to do when someone falls on his face?

First, understand that this person has just been embarrassed and is in need of a friend. So say to that person, "I know how you must feel. I know when I've 'laid an egg' I've been embarrassed." Your care and concern, even if you don't come up with the right words, will be quite a help to the person who is hurting and you will have made a friend in the process.

The bee is more honored than other creatures not because she labors, but because she labors for others.

—St. John Chrysostom

When I was in the first grade in Yazoo City, Mississippi, I had all of the childhood diseases and missed four months of school. There is no doubt in my mind that I would have failed the first grade had it not been for Mrs. Dement Warren, my first-grade teacher. Twice each week she came to our home and spent an hour bringing me up to speed in my lessons and giving me my assignments.

Her "isolated" act of compassion and kindness to me has also impacted the people I've been privileged to know, work with, and influence through my books, tapes, and seminars.

Little things make big differences in every facet of life, so to get the most out of life, give life the little extra that makes the difference between winning and losing.

A hole in the ground is nothing at all, but if you step in it you can fall and break your leg. Careless comments, snide remarks, hurtful statements, or a thoughtless act may seem insignificant at the time, but can cause irreparable damage in the lives of others. Be thoughtful in the "little" things in life, and you will build a solid foundation for enjoying the bigger, better things in life—including good relationships with friends, family, and neighbors.

There are over 100 plays in a football game, but the team who wins is the one whose players give that little extra on each of those 100+ plays.

It's not what happens to you—— it's how you handle what happens to you that counts.

Most of us don't get too excited about flat tires or, for that matter, problems of any kind. It seems they always come at the wrong time. But Domingo Pacheco's life was saved by a flat tire which caused him to miss ValuJet flight 592 that crashed in the Everglades on May 11, 1996.

Who knows what the positive benefits might be when unexpected problems are encountered? The next time something unexpected happens, think about it for a moment. Is it really that bad, or is there a chance that what's happened might, in the long run, be the best thing that's happened to you in a long time?

It is impossible for one man to rob or injure another without at the same time robbing and injuring himself more than anybody else.

—Emerson

The captain of the U.S. Cruiser *Vincennes* made an honest but horrible mistake on July 3, 1988, when he used a missile to shoot down an Iranian airliner, killing all 290 passengers.

However, not everyone in America felt remorseful about the tragedy. Many people carried vividly fresh memories of the cruel treatment of American hostages who had been taken prisoner in Iran.

In the midst of all of this, President Reagan sought to pay compensation to the victims' families. When reporters confronted Mr. Reagan concerning the fact that sending such payment would send the wrong message, Mr. Reagan replied, "I don't ever find compassion a bad precedent."

Do the thing and you shall have the power.

—*Emerson*

There is a group of people in our world who are wild-eyed dreamers. They build "mansions in the sky"—with no foundation. They are forever talking about grandiose plans of what they're going to be doing tomorrow, next year, and in the future. My question for those individuals is, "What did you do yesterday, and what are you doing today?"

Fortunately, our world is filled with people who dream, hope, plan—who constantly are striving to improve themselves, the people around them, and the quality of life for everyone. They are the perennial optimists who hope and believe that the future is going to be even better than the past.

The three great essentials to achieve anything worthwhile are first, hard work, second, stick-to-itiveness, third, common sense.

—*Thomas Edison*

What you did yesterday and what you're doing today are good predictors of what you're going to be doing tomorrow—that is, unless you consciously decide to change.

It is my oft-quoted conviction that you were born to win, but in order to be the winner you were born to be, you must plan to win, prepare to win, and then and only then can you expect to win. There's nothing you can do now about yesterday, but there's a great deal you can do about tomorrow. You are guaranteed a better tomorrow by doing your best today, while developing a plan of action for the tomorrows which lie ahead.

About the Author

Zig Ziglar, one of the most popular communicators of his day, is known as the "Motivators' Motivator." More than three million people have attended Zig's live presentations, and millions of others have been inspired by his training tapes and videos. A prolific author, Zig's books have sold more than four million copies worldwide, and his syndicated column, "Zig Ziglar's Encouraging Word," now appears in newspapers nationwide. His long list of awards includes, "Communicator of the Year," by the Sales and Marketing Executives International. But what makes Zig most proud is being happily married to his wife of fifty years, Jean, whom he lovingly calls "Sugar Baby."

For additional information on seminars, scheduling speaking engagements, or to write the author, please address your correspondence to:

Zig Ziglar
3330 Earhart, Suite 204
Carrollton, Texas 75006-5026

Additional copies of this book and other titles by Zig Ziglar are available from your local bookstore.

Zig Ziglar's Little Instruction Book
What I Learned on the Way to the Top

Honor Books
Tulsa, Oklahoma